GOD'S DESIGN IN OUR WORDS

Copyright © 2025 by Thomas Santos

All rights reserved.

No part of this publication may be reproduced, distributed, or transmitted in any form or by any means, including photocopying, recording, or other electronic or mechanical methods, without the prior written permission of the publisher, except in the case of brief quotations used in critical reviews or certain other noncommercial uses permitted by copyright law.

Copyright registration number: TXu 2-507-0401

Published by ADAPT Publishing

Rancho Santa Margarita, Orange County, California

Edited and designed by Vicki Ramírez Fraga

Scripture quotations taken from the Holy Bible, New International Version®, NIV®. Copyright © 1973, 1978, 1984, 2011 by Biblica, Inc.™ Used by permission. All rights reserved worldwide.

Printed in the United States of America

ISBN: 979-8-9998062-4-6

GOD'S DESIGN IN OUR WORDS

The Bible Behind
the Phrases
We All Use

By
Thomas Santos

CONTENT TABLE

PROLOGUE..7

INTRODUCTION..9

1. "A HOUSE DIVIDED CANNOT STAND"......................11
2. "A LABOR OF LOVE"...15
3. "A LEOPARD CAN'T CHANGE ITS SPOTS"...................19
4. "A DROP IN THE BUCKET".....................................23
5. "AN AYE FOR AN EYE"..27
6. "APPLE OF MY EYE"...31
7. "AS OLD AS METHUSELAH"....................................35
8. "A MAN AFTER MY OWN HEART"............................39
9. "A MULTITUDE OF SINS"..43
10. "A VOICE CRYING IN THE WILDERNESS"....................47
11. "AT THE ELEVENTH HOUR"....................................51
12. "BE A GOOD SAMARITAN".....................................55
13. "BITE THE DUST"...59
14. "BY THE SKIN OF YOUR TEETH"..............................63
15. "CAST THE FIRST STONE".....................................67
16. "EAT, DRINK, AND BE MERRY"................................71
17. "FALL FROM GRACE"..75
18. "FOR EVERYTHING, THERE IS A SEASON"..................79
19. "FIGHT THE GOOD FIGHT"....................................83
20. "FORBIDEN FRUIT"..87

21. "GIVE UP THE GHOST" 91

22. "GO THE EXTRA MILE" 95

23. "HEART OF STONE" 99

24. "THE HANDWRITING ON THE WALL" 103

25. "HOW THE MIGHTY HAVE FALLEN" 107

26. "IN THE TWINKLING OF AN EYE" 111

27. "IN THE BEGINNING" 115

28. "LOVE THY NEIGHBOR AS THYSELF" 119

29. "MANY ARE CALLED, BUT FEW ARE CHOSEN" 123

30. "NO REST FOR THE WICKED" 127

31. "OUT OF THE MOUTHS OF BABES" 131

32. "PRIDE COMES BEFORE A FALL" 135

33. "RISE AND SHINE" 139

34. "SCAPEGOAT" 143

35. "SEEK AND YOU SHALL FIND" 147

36. "THE BLIND LEADING THE BLIND" 151

37. "THE POWERS THAT BE" 155

38. "THE ROOT OF ALL EVIL" 159

39. "THE SALT OF THE EARTH" 163

40. "THE SPIRIT IS WILLING, BUT THE FLESH IS WEAK" 167

CONCLUSION 171

PROLOGUE

The idea for this book started in the most ordinary way—during a Saturday morning Bible study at our local Calvary Chapel in Rancho Santa Margarita, California. My wife and I were going over a workbook our pastor had given us the week before, and as we shared our answers, I couldn't help but notice something: people from all kinds of backgrounds—different ages, experiences, and cultures—kept using the same familiar phrases.

It struck me as both funny and fascinating. These weren't just random sayings. They were clichés—little bits of language we've all heard a thousand times. But sitting there, it hit me: *Where did all of these phrases come from in the first place?*

The thought followed me long after that study ended. I remembered my years in the Navy, traveling around the world. No matter where I went—different countries, different cultures—I still heard those same expressions pop up. Later, as I traveled in civilian life, the pattern kept repeating itself. And then it finally clicked: so many of these everyday sayings trace back to one common source—the Bible.

That realization became the seed for this book. Think about it: God's Word has influenced languages, cultures, and societies all over the globe—so much so that people quote Scripture without even knowing it. The Bible has left its fingerprints on the way we talk, and that says something powerful about its reach and relevance.

But there's more. These phrases don't just tell us where our words come from—they can also open doors. A cliché can be a surprisingly natural way to bring God into a conversation. It's a starting point, a gentle bridge. Instead of forcing a deep talk out of nowhere, you can connect with someone through a phrase they already know:

- **IT'S RELATABLE.** Say "Everything happens for a reason," and suddenly you're connecting to the shared longing for purpose. From there, you can point to God's plan.
- **IT'S NON-THREATENING.** Quoting "It's in God's hands" feels gentle, not pushy. It opens the door without making someone defensive.
- **IT'S SHARED WISDOM.** "Do unto others..." isn't just good advice—it's straight from Jesus, and it lets you show that the Bible has already shaped what people value.
- **IT'S A BRIDGE.** "The best is yet to come" can lead right into hope, heaven, and God's promises.
- **IT'S COMFORTING.** "God works in mysterious ways" may sound simple, but it reminds people that they're not alone—that there's Someone bigger at work.

That's what this book is about: rediscovering the biblical roots of phrases we've been saying all our lives, and learning how to use them as steppingstones to share God's truth.

I've even left space in the margins for you to jot down your own thoughts, questions, and ideas. My prayer is that as you read, you won't just learn a few fun facts—you'll see fresh opportunities to talk about God in everyday life.

INTRODUCTION

The Bible has shaped the world in more ways than we can count. It's in our art, our laws, our values—and, maybe most surprisingly, in our everyday conversations. Words that first showed up in ancient Hebrew and Greek are now sprinkled across English, Spanish, and countless other languages. You hear them in classrooms, in courtrooms, in movies, in songs, and even around the dinner table.

Most of the time, we don't even notice.

We say, "By the skin of my teeth," when we barely make it through. We shake our heads at a politician and mutter, "How the mighty have fallen." We cheer each other on with, "Fight the good fight." And yet, few of us stop to ask—where did those words actually come from?

The answer: straight out of the Bible.

For centuries, Scripture has quietly woven itself into culture. Shakespeare borrowed it for his plays. Leaders and activists leaned on it to fuel speeches that stirred nations. Artists painted its stories. Teachers used its parables to shape lessons. Even today, when people call for justice, compassion, or forgiveness, they often lean on biblical language to give their words weight.

And it's not just for politics or classrooms. The Bible has been a source of comfort, too. How many times has someone whispered, "God works in mysterious ways," at a funeral, or "Love covers a multitude of sins," when a relationship needed mending? These words remind us of something bigger—that behind life's chaos, there's a God who sees, loves, and cares.

The truth is, the Bible's influence runs deep.

In literature: Shakespeare wasn't the only one—writers for

centuries have echoed Scripture, making it part of our shared imagination.

In ethics and law: Words about justice, mercy, and human dignity shaped entire legal systems and continue to guide debates today.

In politics and social movements: From abolitionists to civil rights leaders, biblical phrases gave courage to stand for freedom and equality.

In culture and media: Movies, music, and even TV sitcoms drop in biblical language like inside jokes we all somehow recognize.

In schools: Generations of students grew up reading its stories, wrestling with its lessons, and letting it shape their ideas of right and wrong.

In everyday talk: Whether we know it or not, most of us quote the Bible every week—sometimes every day.

And here's the twist: over time, a lot of these phrases drifted from their original meaning. They became slogans, clichés, throwaway lines. But go back to the source, and you'll see they're far from shallow—they carry stories, warnings, promises, and hope.

That's what this book is about. We're going to dust off those sayings, set them back in their biblical context, and see what they really mean. You'll laugh at how familiar they are. You'll be surprised at how relevant they still feel. And you'll realize that Scripture hasn't just shaped history—it's been shaping your life all along, even in the words you speak without thinking.

So here's your invitation: read with curiosity. Scribble in the margins. Have fun with it. Share what you learn with friends. Let these old clichés surprise you, challenge you, and remind you that the Bible isn't outdated—it's alive, powerful, and still shaping the way we see the world today.

① "A HOUSE DIVIDED CANNOT STAND"

(WHAT DO HOUSES HAVE TO DO WITH ARGUMENTS?)

YOU MIGHT'VE HEARD SOMEONE SAY...

"A HOUSE DIVIDED AGAINST ITSELF CANNOT STAND."

Maybe it was during a *political debate*, a *family conflict*, or even on a history documentary (yep, Abraham Lincoln made it famous too).

It's a serious-sounding phrase—used when **things are falling apart** because people just can't seem to get along.

But most people don't know that this isn't just a smart quote or a political slogan...
It's something Jesus said.

❓ WHERE IT COMES FROM

This phrase comes from Jesus himself in Matthew 12:25:

> "Every kingdom divided against itself is laid waste, and no city or house divided against itself will stand."

The context? Jesus had just healed a man, and the religious leaders accused Him of using evil powers. He responded with this famous line, showing the absurdity: how can a kingdom or a household fight itself and survive?

His message is clear: division destroys. Whether it's a nation, a church, or a family—if it tears itself apart, it won't stand.

⭐ A FAMOUS REUSE

Hundreds of years later, Abraham Lincoln used this phrase in his famous "HOUSE DIVIDED" *speech* during a time of deep tension in the United States over *slavery*.

He reminded the country that it couldn't survive if it stayed divided.

The quote has stuck ever since.

But long before it echoed through history books, it was a reminder from Jesus: **Unity matters.**

🪴 WHY IT MATTERS

We live in a divided world. Families, churches, friendships, even nations split over pride, opinions, and power struggles. But Jesus didn't just warn us about division—**He came to heal it.**

When we love like *He loves*, when we forgive like *He forgives*, when we stand *together*—that's when the "house" becomes strong again.

🧠 THINK ABOUT IT

▶ Is there division in your "house"—your heart, family, or friendships?

_____
_____
_____
_____
_____

▶ What could you do to bring peace instead of more cracks?

_____
_____
_____
_____
_____

🫶 TRY THIS

Next time someone says, "A HOUSE DIVIDED CAN'T STAND," you can gently respond:

> "That's actually something Jesus said. It's a powerful reminder that unity really matters to God."

A simple phrase… that might lead to a deeper talk.

2
"A LABOR OF LOVE"
(IS IT REALLY WORK IF YOU LOVE IT?)

YOU MIGHT'VE HEARD SOMEONE SAY...

"IT'S A LABOR OF LOVE."

It usually comes up when someone is working really hard on something—but they're not getting paid, or they're not doing it for applause.

Think of a mom making birthday cupcakes at 2 a.m. A grandpa building a toy box for the grandkids. A teacher staying late to help a struggling student.

No one's forcing them. They do it because they care. That's what we call a labor of love.

WHERE IT COMES FROM

This phrase comes from 1 Thessalonians 1:3:

> "We remember before our God and Father your work produced by faith, your labor prompted by love, and your endurance inspired by hope in our Lord Jesus Christ."

Paul was commending the believers for a faith that worked, a love that served, and a hope that endured. Their devotion wasn't just words—it showed up in action. That's the heart behind the phrase: **love that rolls up its sleeves.**

⭐ MORE THAN JUST HARD WORK

Today, "A LABOR OF LOVE" describes any work done because you care—not because you have to. Sewing quilts for a hospital? *Labor of love.* Starting a little free library in your neighborhood? *Labor of love.* Writing a book to help others grow in faith? You guessed it.

But in Scripture, it's not just about effort—it's about motive. Love is what turns ordinary work into *something eternal.* When we serve out of love for God and others, the work may be tiring, but *it's never wasted.*

🪴 WHY IT MATTERS

We live in a world that often measures value by results, money, or recognition. But *God looks at the heart.*

A **task done in love** carries more weight than any achievement done in pride. Jesus showed us the greatest labor of love when He gave His life for us. His sacrifice reminds us that love is proven through action, not applause.

Following Him means **choosing to love through action**, even when no one sees, trusting that He notices and delights in every act of faithfulness.

THINK ABOUT IT

- What's something hard you've done—not because you had to, but because you loved someone?

_____
_____
_____
_____

- What could you do today that would be a labor of love for someone else?

_____
_____
_____
_____

TRY THIS

Next time someone says, "IT'S A LABOR OF LOVE," you could say:

"You know, that phrase comes from the Bible—Paul used it to describe the kind of love that shows up and gets to work!"

A perfect way to share God's love in a natural conversation.

3
"A LEOPARD CAN'T CHANGE ITS SPOTS"
(IS CHANGE EVEN POSSIBLE?)

YOU MIGHT'VE HEARD SOMEONE SAY...

"WELL, A LEOPARD CAN'T CHANGE ITS SPOTS."

Usually it means something like, "PEOPLE NEVER REALLY CHANGE." It's a phrase used when someone messes up again—or when we assume someone will always stay the same, especially if they've done wrong.

But did you know it comes from the Bible?
And the way it's used there... is actually a little intense.

WHERE IT COMES FROM

This phrase appears in Jeremiah 13:23:

> "Can an Ethiopian change his skin or a leopard its spots? Neither can you do good who are accustomed to doing evil."

That's a heavy verse. Through Jeremiah, God was speaking to people who had repeatedly turned from Him. They were stuck in sin and unwilling to change. The point wasn't to mock them—but to show how deeply sin takes root when we ignore God.

Like a leopard can't scrub off its spots, people can't cleanse their hearts on their own.

⭐ SO... CAN PEOPLE REALLY CHANGE?

Here's the good news:

Yes—but not on our own.

We can't erase sin with good behavior or self-effort. But **God can change us from the inside out.**

Jesus didn't come to make bad people behave better— He came to make **dead hearts come alive.**

So, even though a leopard can't change its spots, **God can change a heart.**

🪴 WHY IT MATTERS

Don't believe the lie that you'll always be the same.

Yes—some struggles go deep.

Yes—patterns can be hard to break.

But *you are not your past.* You're not your worst day. You're not defined by the failures that others remember, or the shame you carry in silence.

The world may say, "PEOPLE NEVER CHANGE," but the gospel says, "IF ANYONE IS IN CHRIST, HE IS A NEW CREATION." God doesn't just improve you—He gives you a brand-new heart.

 THINK ABOUT IT

- Have you ever wanted to "get even"?

  _____
  _____
  _____
  _____
  _____

- What would it look like to go beyond that—and forgive?

  _____
  _____
  _____
  _____
  _____

♡ TRY THIS

Next time someone says, "AN EYE FOR AN EYE," try asking:

> "Do you know where that comes from? Actually, it was a law meant to stop revenge. And Jesus offered a better way—grace."

You might be surprised how open people are to the conversation!

4
"A DROP IN THE BUCKET"
(TINY THINGS IN A BIG PICTURE)

YOU MIGHT'VE HEARD SOMEONE SAY...

"IT'S JUST A DROP IN THE BUCKET."

People usually say it when something feels small compared to something huge like: "I DONATED, BUT IT'S JUST A DROP IN THE BUCKET.", or "ONE VOICE IN THE CROWD? DROP IN THE BUCKET."

It's their way of saying: THAT BARELY MADE A DIFFERENCE.

Later on, the phrase grew into **"a drop in the ocean"**—same idea, just a bigger picture.

But here's the twist: the phrase actually comes from the Bible—and it's not about discouragement... it's about perspective.

❓ WHERE IT COMES FROM

This phrase comes from *Isaiah 40:15*:

> "Surely the nations are like a drop in a bucket; they are regarded as dust on the scales; he weighs the islands as though they were fine dust."

In other words, all the power of the world's nations—armies, empires, rulers, kingdoms—are tiny when compared to the greatness of God.

A single drop in a big, heavy bucket barely matters. It's **insignificant.** And Isaiah's point is this: **Nothing on earth compares to God.**

His power, His wisdom, His greatness—it's unmatched.

 BUT DOES THAT MEAN WE DON'T MATTER?

Not at all.

Isaiah's point isn't that you're worthless.

It's that God is limitless.

Yes—compared to Him, we are small. But this same all-powerful God also calls us His children.

He sees every tear.

He hears every prayer.

He knows every hair on your head.

So while the nations may be a drop in the bucket...

you're the apple of His eye.

 WHY IT MATTERS

We often think our problems—or even the world's problems—are too big to solve. But Isaiah flips the view: next to God, even the mightiest challenges are "BUCKET DROPS."

That should humble us when we think we're in control, and comfort us when we feel outnumbered or overwhelmed.

And when your own effort feels small—like your prayer, your act of kindness, your tiny bit of faith—it's not wasted.

Drops matter when God is the One holding the bucket.

🧠 THINK ABOUT IT

▶ What's one "giant" in your life that feels too big to face?

_____
_____
_____
_____
_____

▶ How does seeing it as "just a drop" compared to God's greatness change things?

_____
_____
_____
_____
_____

💗 TRY THIS

Next time someone says, "IT'S JUST A DROP IN THE BUCKET," say this:

> "That's from the Bible! It's a reminder that even the biggest things on earth are tiny next to God… and yet He still sees and values us."

That one sentence might plant a powerful seed.

5

"AN AYE FOR AN EYE"

(IS THAT REALLY ABOUT REVENGE?)

YOU MIGHT'VE HEARD SOMEONE SAY...

"WELL, IT'S JUST AN EYE FOR AN EYE."

People usually say it when they want payback—like, "YOU HIT ME, I'LL HIT YOU BACK."

But what if we told you this phrase was never about getting even... but about stopping things from getting worse?

Yup—it comes straight from the Bible...

❓ WHERE IT COMES FROM

The phrase is found in Exodus 21:24:

> "Eye for eye, tooth for tooth, hand for hand, foot for foot."

This was part of the Mosaic Law, called lex talionis—the law of retaliation. In the ancient world, people often took revenge too far. If someone knocked out your tooth, you might burn down their house. God gave this law not to promote violence, but to limit it. It was a safeguard to ensure the punishment matched the crime—justice with boundaries.

⭐ WHAT JESUS SAID

Years later, Jesus spoke about this very law in Matthew 5:38–39. But He flipped it upside down.

> "You have heard that it was said, 'Eye for eye, and tooth for tooth.' But I tell you, do not resist an evil person. If someone slaps you on the right cheek, turn to them the other also."

Jesus didn't cancel justice—He showed a new way: grace. **Instead of giving people what they deserve, we can give them what they don't:** patience, mercy, forgiveness. Why? Because that's what God gives us.

🪴 WHY IT MATTERS

We all know what it feels like to want payback. When someone hurts us, our instinct is to strike back harder, to make them feel what we felt. But revenge only keeps the cycle of pain going. God's law put a boundary on that cycle, and Jesus went even further—He broke it with grace.

Choosing patience and forgiveness doesn't make you weak; it makes you free. It frees you from bitterness, frees you from being controlled by someone else's actions, and points others to the mercy of Christ. In a world that shouts "Get even," Jesus invites us to live differently: to show the same mercy we've been given.

🧠 THINK ABOUT IT

▸ Have you ever wanted to "get even"?

_____
_____
_____
_____

▸ What would it look like to go beyond that—and forgive?

_____
_____
_____
_____

🫱 TRY THIS

Next time someone says, "AN EYE FOR AN EYE," try asking:

"Do you know where that comes from? Actually, it was a law meant to stop revenge. And Jesus offered a better way—grace."

You might be surprised how open people are to the conversation!

6
"APPLE OF MY EYE"
(WAIT... WHAT'S FRUIT GOT TO DO WITH IT?)

YOU MIGHT'VE HEARD SOMEONE SAY...

"SHE'S THE APPLE OF MY EYE."

It sounds sweet, right? We usually say it about someone we deeply love—like a child, a best friend, or even a pet. It means they're precious to us, one of a kind.

But... have you ever wondered why an apple? And more importantly—where this phrase even comes from?

Surprise! It comes from the Bible. And it doesn't actually refer to fruit at all.

❓ WHERE IT COMES FROM

The phrase shows up in Deuteronomy 32:10, in a song of God's care for His people:

> "He found him in a desert land, and in the howling waste of the wilderness; He encircled him, He cared for him, He kept him as the apple of His eye."

Here, *"the apple of His eye"* is a poetic way of saying, **"You are My most treasured possession."** It describes God's deep, personal love for Israel—His chosen people.

☆ THE SPOT WE PROTECT MOST

In Hebrew, the phrase refers to the pupil of the eye—the most delicate part of the body, instinctively guarded and protected. Just blink when something flies toward your face—you'll do anything to shield that tiny spot.

That's the image: God is alert, tender, and fiercely protective over His people, guarding what *He loves most*.

🪴 WHY IT MATTERS

This isn't just about a pretty metaphor—it's about how God sees you. You are not a mistake. You are not forgotten. You are not too small, too late, or too broken.

To God, you are the apple of His eye—the one He treasures, guards, and loves beyond measure. And when you know you are that deeply loved, it changes how you see yourself and how you walk through life.

THINK ABOUT IT

▸ Who in your life makes you feel deeply loved and protected?

_____
_____
_____
_____

▸ What if God's love for you is even stronger than that?

_____
_____
_____
_____

TRY THIS

Next time someone says, "HE'S THE APPLE OF MY EYE," you could say:

> "Did you know that's actually from the Bible? God used it to describe how much He cares for us!"

A perfect way to share God's love in a natural conversation.

7
"AS OLD AS METHUSELAH"
(OKAY... BUT WHO WAS METHUSELAH?)

YOU MIGHT'VE HEARD SOMEONE SAY...

"HE'S AS OLD AS METHUSELAH!"

...usually followed by a laugh.

It's a playful way of saying someone (or something) is really, really old. But most people have no idea who Methuselah was—or why his name became the go-to symbol for extreme age.

Spoiler: he was a real person in the Bible. And yes... he was *really, really old.*

[?] WHERE IT COMES FROM

You can find Methuselah's name in the first book of the Bible—Genesis 5:27:

> "Altogether, Methuselah lived a total of 969 years, and then he died."

Yep. 969 years. That makes him the **oldest person recorded in the Bible**—and in all of history, according to Scripture.

Methuselah was the son of Enoch (who famously "walked with God") and the grandfather of Noah (yes, that Noah—the one with the ark). Though the Bible doesn't tell us much about his personality or life, his age became legendary.

⭐ MORE THAN A FUN FACT

Over time, the phrase "AS OLD AS METHUSELAH" became a humorous idiom, used to exaggerate age. People might say a very old car is "AS OLD AS METHUSELAH," or that a grandma's cookie recipe has been "AROUND SINCE METHUSELAH'S TIME."

But behind the humor is something fascinating: Methuselah's life represents patience. According to the biblical timeline, he died the very year the flood came. Some believe this was God's way of holding back judgment—giving humanity as much time as possible to turn back to Him.

🪴 WHY IT MATTERS

Methuselah reminds us that long life is a gift, but it's what we do with our time that really counts.

Whether you live to be 100 or 969...

- Did you *walk with God*?

- Did you leave a *legacy of faith*?

- Did you *help others* know Him?

Old age isn't the goal.

Walking with God is.

🗨 THINK ABOUT IT

▶ If God gave you 969 years... What would you do with them?

_____
_____
_____
_____
_____

▶ What can you do today that will matter for eternity?

_____
_____
_____
_____
_____

🫶 TRY THIS

The next time someone jokes, "I FEEL AS OLD AS METHUSELAH!" You can say:

"He was actually a guy in the Bible—he lived 969 years! But what's really cool is what that says about God's patience."

Boom—conversation started.

8
"A MAN AFTER MY OWN HEART"
(IS THIS A COMPLIMENT?)

YOU MIGHT'VE HEARD SOMEONE SAY...

"HE'S A MAN AFTER MY OWN HEART."

We hear this phrase all the time. It's usually a compliment—like when two people discover they both love the same music, food, or sense of humor.

- A dad sees his son grab a slice of pizza with extra pepperoni and smiles, "THAT'S A MAN AFTER MY OWN HEART."
- Two friends laugh over the same cheesy movie, and one says, "SEE? YOU GET ME. YOU'RE AFTER MY OWN HEART."

In everyday life, it's our way of saying, "We think alike. We share the same passions. You *understand me.*"

But did you know the phrase originally came from the Bible? And in that context, it means something *way deeper.*

❓ WHERE IT COMES FROM

In **1 Samuel 13:14,** the prophet Samuel tells King Saul:

> "But now your kingdom will not endure; the Lord has sought out a man after his own heart and appointed him ruler of his people..."

That "man after God's own heart" was David. But why? He wasn't the oldest, strongest, or most qualified. In fact, he was the youngest of his brothers—a shepherd boy with a slingshot.

But what set David apart wasn't his talent. It was his heart. He loved God. He trusted God. He wanted to please God, even when he messed up. David's life wasn't perfect, but his heart stayed soft toward the Lord.

⭐ SHARING GOD'S HEART

Today, when someone says, "HE'S A MAN AFTER MY OWN HEART," they usually mean:

"WE'RE ON THE SAME PAGE. WE CARE ABOUT THE SAME THINGS."

So when the Bible says David was a man after God's own heart, it means:

"He wants what God wants. He cares about what God cares about."

What a powerful way to live.

🪴 WHY IT MATTERS

God isn't looking for perfection.

He's looking for **devotion**.

That means your **gifts**, your **mistake**s, your **story**—all of it—can still bring joy to God's heart if you're walking in love, humility, and trust.

You don't have to be the best.

Just be someone who says:

"God, I want to know You. I want to follow You."

That's the kind of heart He loves.

🧠 THINK ABOUT IT

- If someone looked at your life, would they say: *"That's someone after God's heart"*?

_____
_____
_____
_____

- What's one small thing you could do today to grow that kind of heart?

_____
_____
_____
_____

🫶 TRY THIS

If you hear someone say, "HE'S A MAN AFTER MY OWN HEART," you can say:

"That's actually a phrase from the Bible! It's what God said about King David—a man who truly loved Him."

Simple comment. Eternal truth.

9
"A MULTITUDE OF SINS"
(CAN LOVE REALLY COVER THAT MUCH?)

YOU MIGHT'VE HEARD SOMEONE SAY...

"WELL.. LOVE COVERS A MULTITUDE OF SINS."

It's often said with a smile—maybe after someone burns dinner or forgets a birthday.

It's a gentle way of saying, *"It's okay. I still love you."*

But that little phrase isn't just a poetic way to excuse mistakes.

It comes from the Bible—and it's much more powerful than most people realize.

[?] WHERE IT COMES FROM

In 1 Peter 4:8, the apostle Peter writes:

> "Above all, love each other deeply, because love covers over a multitude of sins."

He was writing to early Christians going through serious challenges—persecution, pressure, misunderstandings. And what did he tell them?

Love each other. Deeply.
Why? Because **love has the power to heal.**

When we truly love others, we forgive more freely. We let go of offenses. We show grace, even when it's hard.

⭐ MORE THAN A HALLMARK CARD

This isn't just "romantic" love or good feelings.

It's **sacrificial love.** The kind that sees the worst in someone... and chooses to stay.

The kind of love that says:

> "I know you messed up—but I still see you. I still care. I'm not going anywhere."

That's the kind of love that changes hearts. That kind of love?

It looks a lot like Jesus.

🪴 WHY IT MATTERS

We all mess up. We all say things we wish we hadn't. We all carry scars—some we gave, some we received. But love—real love—has the power to cover, to forgive, and to heal.

This doesn't mean pretending nothing happened. It means choosing to respond to sin with mercy, not revenge.

When we love deeply, we create space for people to grow and for relationships to be restored.

🧠 THINK ABOUT IT

▸ Is there someone in your life who needs grace today?

_____
_____
_____
_____

▸ What would it look like to love them—not because they earned it, but because you've been loved, too?

_____
_____
_____
_____

🫶 TRY THIS

If someone says, "WELL, LOVE COVERS A MULTITUDE OF SINS," you can gently respond:

"That's actually from the Bible—and it's such a beautiful truth. Love doesn't excuse sin, but it helps heal what sin has broken."

You never know who might need to hear that.

"A VOICE CRYING IN THE WILDERNESS"

(CAN ONE VOICE MAKE A DIFFERENCE?)

YOU MIGHT'VE HEARD SOMEONE SAY...

"IT'S LIKE A VOICE CRYING IN THE WILDERNESS."

It's usually said when someone feels unheard—like their warnings or advice are falling on deaf ears. Think of someone saying something important... but no one's listening.

The phrase sounds poetic—but its roots are powerful.

It comes from the Bible, and it's directly connected to a bold, strange prophet with wild hair and a fierce message: **John the Baptist.**

WHERE IT COMES FROM

This phrase is found in **Isaiah 40:3:**

"A voice of one calling: 'In the wilderness prepare the way for the Lord; make straight in the desert a highway for our God.'"

Hundreds of years later, the New Testament tells us this verse was about John the Baptist—a man God chose to prepare the way for Jesus.

He lived in the desert, wore camel hair, ate locusts and honey, and had one mission: tell people to get ready for the Messiah. His message was radical, calling people to turn from sin and back to God. Not everyone liked it—many mocked him—but his voice in a dry, distracted world was exactly what God used.

⭐ SPEAKING UP WHEN NO ONE LISTENS

Now, when people say someone is "A VOICE CRYING IN THE WILDERNESS," they usually mean:

> "That person is speaking truth, even though no one's listening."

It's often used for brave souls who **stand up for justice**, speak hard truths, or call people back to what's right—even when it's unpopular.

Think of a whistleblower exposing corruption, a teacher urging kindness when cruelty is easier, or a friend telling you the hard truth you didn't want to hear. Their words may *not be popular*, but they're needed. Like John the Baptist, their *"voice"* cuts through the noise, pointing back to what really matters.

🪴 WHY IT MATTERS

Sometimes *it feels like* our words or actions don't matter. Maybe you've stood up for what's right and got ignored, shared your faith and felt dismissed, or tried to do the right thing and ended up feeling alone.

But here's the truth: God hears every faithful voice. And sometimes the world needs your voice—even if it doesn't realize it yet. Don't underestimate the power of one voice, speaking in love and truth.

🗣 THINK ABOUT IT

- Has there ever been a moment when you felt like no one was listening to what really mattered?

  _____
  _____
  _____
  _____
  _____

- What would it look like to speak the truth anyway—with courage and kindness?

  _____
  _____
  _____
  _____
  _____

🫶 TRY THIS

Next time someone says, "IT'S LIKE A VOICE IN THE WILDERNESS" you can say:

> "That's actually a phrase from Isaiah—and later used to describe John the Baptist. He spoke truth when no one else would."

Who knows? **That might be the voice someone needs to hear.**

11
"AT THE ELEVENTH HOUR"
(IS IT TOO LATE?)

YOU MIGHT'VE HEARD SOMEONE SAY...

"THEY SHOWED UP AT THE ELEVENTH HOUR,"

what they usually mean is:
"They waited until the very last moment."

The phrase is often used when someone finishes something just before a deadline—or makes a big change right before time runs out.

But before it was a deadline cliché, this phrase was part of **a story Jesus told about grace, generosity, and unexpected mercy.**

⌕ WHERE IT COMES FROM

The phrase comes from one of Jesus' parables in Matthew 20. A landowner went out early in the morning to hire workers for his vineyard. As the day went on, he returned again at 9 a.m., noon, 3 p.m., and finally at 5 p.m.—the eleventh hour—and brought in more workers.

When evening came, he surprised everyone by paying each person the same wage, even those who had only worked an hour.

The full-day workers grumbled, "THAT'S NOT FAIR!" But the landowner answered, "I'm not being unfair—I'm being generous."

 WHAT IT MEANS TODAY

Today, "at the eleventh hour" just means something happened really late—*almost too late.*

But in Jesus' story, the phrase points to something far greater: **it's never too late to say yes to God.**

Even those who showed up "last minute" still received the full reward—not because they earned it, but because of the landowner's generosity.

His point is clear: God's grace isn't measured by hours on the clock but by His heart of mercy.

 WHY IT MATTERS

This parable reminds us that God is far more generous than we imagine.

- Maybe you've wandered for years...
- Maybe you feel like you're too late to change...
- Maybe others made it to the vineyard before you...

But here's the good news:

If you come to God—even at the eleventh hour—He welcomes you with open arms.

God doesn't keep score the way we do. His kingdom runs on **grace**, not comparison.

🗣 THINK ABOUT IT

▸ Have you ever felt like it was too late to start over?

_____
_____
_____
_____
_____

▸ What if God is still inviting you in—even now?

_____
_____
_____
_____
_____

🫶 TRY THIS

If someone says, "WELL, THEY CAME IN AT THE ELEVENTH HOUR," you can say:

"That phrase actually comes from a parable Jesus told—it's a beautiful reminder that God's grace is never too late."

12
"BE A GOOD SAMARITAN"
(WHAT IF KINDNESS IS THE POINT?)

YOU MIGHT'VE HEARD SOMEONE SAY...

"WOW, WHAT A GOOD SAMARITAN!"

We say it when someone helps a stranger—changing a flat tire, paying for groceries, or stepping in during a crisis. It's a way of saying, "That person cared when they didn't have to."

But the phrase comes from one of Jesus' most famous stories—a parable that shocked His listeners, flipped cultural expectations, and asked a bigger question: Who is my neighbor? It's not just about random good deeds, but about mercy that crosses barriers and shows God's love in action.

[?] WHERE IT COMES FROM

The story comes from Luke 10:25–37. When a lawyer asked Jesus, **"What must I do to inherit eternal life?"** Jesus turned the question back: **"What does the Law say?"** The man replied, **"Love God and love your neighbor."** Wanting to *justify* himself, he asked, **"And who is my neighbor?"**

So Jesus told a parable: A man was beaten and left for dead. A priest and a Levite saw him but passed by. Finally, a Samaritan—an outsider to the Jewish audience—stopped. He treated the man's wounds, carried him on his donkey, and paid for his stay at an inn.

Then Jesus asked, "Who was the neighbor?" The lawyer answered, *"The one who showed mercy."*

Jesus said, "Go and do likewise."

☆ MORE THAN JUST HELPING

Being a *"Good Samaritan"* isn't just about doing nice things.

It's about **seeing people**—especially the ones we might overlook or avoid.

It's about choosing compassion when it's inconvenient.

It's about crossing boundaries, breaking prejudice, and loving without conditions.

It's a radical kind of kindness—one that looks a lot like Jesus.

🪴 WHY IT MATTERS

In a world that rushes past the wounded, in a culture that says "you do you" and "mind your own business," Jesus calls us to stop, see, and serve.

The call to **"be a good Samaritan"** is a call to love our neighbors—**even when it costs us something.**

THINK ABOUT IT

▶ Have you ever walked past someone in need—because it felt too inconvenient?

_____
_____
_____
_____
_____

▶ What would it look like to "go and do likewise" this week?

_____
_____
_____
_____
_____

TRY THIS

If someone says, "SHE'S A REAL GOOD SAMARITAN," you can say:

"That's actually a story Jesus told—it's a beautiful picture of what love in action looks like."

You might open a door to a deeper conversation about mercy, kindness, and Christ.

13
"BITE THE DUST"
(YOU MEAN LIKE... DIRT?)

YOU MIGHT'VE HEARD SOMEONE SAY...

"ANOTHER ONE BITES THE DUST..."

Whether you've heard it in a song, a western movie, or on the playground, this phrase has become a classic way to say someone just lost big time.

Maybe their plan failed. Maybe their team lost. Maybe they face-planted trying a backflip.

"WELL.. HE BIT THE DUST."

We say it half-jokingly now. But the roots of this phrase? They're actually found in one of the earliest moments of the Bible.

❓ WHERE IT COMES FROM

The idea of "biting the dust" comes from Genesis 3:19, when God speaks to Adam after he and Eve disobeyed:

> "By the sweat of your brow you will eat your food until you return to the ground, since from it you were taken; for dust you are and to dust you will return."

This wasn't just a poetic way of talking about hard work or death—it was the moment when sin entered the world, and with it, pain, toil, and mortality.

The phrase "to dust you will return" is a reminder of our human limits—our brokenness, our fragility, and our deep need for God.

⭐ FROM SERIOUS TO SLANG

Over time, the image of falling down into the dust became a symbol for defeat.

- A warrior falling in battle
- A runner collapsing from exhaustion
- A plan crashing to the ground

So eventually, "BITE THE DUST" became a way to say:

"They lost. They failed. They're done."

It's funny now—but the meaning still echoes a deeper truth.

🪴 WHY IT MATTERS

"Biting the dust" is part of the human story.

We fall. We mess up. We return to the ground.

But that's not where the story ends.

Jesus came into our dusty world, took on our failure, and offered us life.

Because of Him, even though we came from dust... **we don't have to stay there.**

 THINK ABOUT IT

▶ What's a time when you "bit the dust"?

_____
_____
_____
_____
_____

▶ How did you get back up—and what helped you move forward?

_____
_____
_____
_____
_____

🫶 TRY THIS

If someone jokes, "WELL, I BIT THE DUST," you could say:

"You know that's actually from the Bible? It's a reminder that we all fall—but God can lift us up again."

Sometimes humor can lead to hope.

14
"BY THE SKIN OF YOUR TEETH"
(THAT WAS WAY TOO CLOSE)

YOU MIGHT'VE HEARD SOMEONE SAY...

"I MADE IT... BY THE SKIN OF MY TEETH!"

It usually means someone barely made it through—like a narrow escape or a close call.

- Just passing a test.
- Just making it to the airport.
- Just avoiding something going terribly wrong.

But the phrase actually comes from one of the most intense books in the Bible—Job—and it describes a moment of deep, painful survival.

❓ WHERE IT COMES FROM

In *Job 19:19–20*, Job is speaking out of his suffering:

> "All my intimate friends detest me; those I love have turned against me. I am nothing but skin and bones; I have escaped only by the skin of my teeth."

Job had lost everything—his wealth, his health, his children, and the support of his friends. His body was broken. His spirit was crushed. He was barely hanging on.

That line—*"BY THE SKIN OF MY TEETH"*—is Job's poetic way of saying:

"I'm still alive... but just barely."

WHAT IT MEANS TODAY

Over time, the phrase "BY THE SKIN OF YOUR TEETH" became a way to describe a **narrow escape**—when you come through something difficult by the slimmest margin.

It's used in everyday moments... but originally, it came from a man who had lost almost everything.

So when we use it, we're actually echoing a cry from one of the rawest, most human voices in Scripture.

WHY IT MATTERS

We all face moments where we barely make it.

- Physically.
- Emotionally.
- Spiritually.

Sometimes you survive the day... but only *just*.

Here's the good news: **God is still there—even in the narrow escape.**

Even when you feel like you're barely holding on, He's holding you.

Job's story reminds us that even when everything else falls apart, God is not done writing our story.

 THINK ABOUT IT

▶ Have you ever had a "skin of your teeth" moment—where you barely made it through?

_____
_____
_____
_____
_____

▶ What helped you keep going?

_____
_____
_____
_____
_____

TRY THIS

If someone says, "I MADE IT BY THE SKIN OF MY TEETH," you can say:

> "That's actually a line from Job—he said it when he was hanging on by a thread. But God didn't let go of him."

And God won't let go of you either.

15

"CAST THE FIRST STONE"

(WHO ARE WE TO JUDGE?)

YOU MIGHT'VE HEARD SOMEONE SAY...

"WELL, WHO ARE YOU TO CAST THE FIRST STONE?"

It's usually said when someone is being overly critical or judgmental—as if to say, *"You're not perfect either."*

Today, it's used to caution people against harsh judgment.

But this phrase comes directly from one of Jesus' **most compassionate and disarming moments**—a moment where He defended someone not with anger, but with quiet, soul-piercing truth.

❓ WHERE IT COMES FROM

In John 8:7, a group of religious leaders brought Jesus a woman caught in adultery.

According to the Law of Moses, she deserved to be stoned—but their real goal was to trap Him. If He showed mercy, He'd seem to break the law; if He upheld the law, He'd look heartless.

Instead of arguing, He wrote in the dirt, then said, "Let any one of you who is without sin be the first to throw a stone."

Silence fell. One by one, the accusers slipped away. Only Jesus remained. He turned to the woman and asked, "Has no one condemned you?" "No one, sir," she answered. "Then neither do I condemn you," He replied. "Go now and leave your life of sin."

⭐ LOOK IN THE MIRROR FIRST

Today, "CAST THE FIRST STONE" is a way of saying, "**Don't be so quick to judge**—especially when you've got your own flaws." We use it when someone is harsh on others but blind to their own mistakes. It's a reminder we all need: *every one of us is broken, every one of us needs grace.*

Think about how easy it is to gossip about a coworker's failure while ignoring our own, or to blast someone online for a mistake we've also made.

Often, the loudest critics are the ones hiding the deepest struggles.

🪴 WHY IT MATTERS

Jesus didn't say the woman was innocent. He simply reminded everyone of something deeper:

No one is qualified to throw stones—except Him.
And He chose mercy instead.

This doesn't mean sin is okay. It means **people matter more.** It means we're called to restore, not condemn.

If Jesus—the only sinless one—chose to forgive... what does that say about how we should treat each other?

🗣 THINK ABOUT IT

▸ Have you ever caught yourself being quick to judge someone else?

_____
_____
_____
_____

▸ What would happen if you paused—and offered grace instead?

_____
_____
_____
_____

🫶 TRY THIS

Next time someone says, "DON'T CAST THE FIRST STONE," you can say:

> "That's something Jesus actually said— to stop a group from stoning a woman. It's one of the most powerful examples of compassion in the Bible."

One moment of truth... one open door.

16
"EAT, DRINK, AND BE MERRY"
(IS IT OKAY TO ENJOY LIFE?)

YOU MIGHT'VE HEARD SOMEONE SAY...

"EAT, DRINK, AND BE MERRY!"

We say it at parties, celebrations, or when life just feels good. It's a fun phrase—one that sounds like a toast. And today, people use it when they want to celebrate or enjoy the moment, often without thinking too hard about tomorrow.

But it actually comes from the Bible—from a book of **deep wisdom and hard questions.**

❓ WHERE IT COMES FROM

The phrase comes from Ecclesiastes 8:15, where the author, traditionally believed to be Solomon, writes:

> "So I commend the enjoyment of life, because there is nothing better for a person under the sun than to eat and drink and be glad. Then joy will accompany them in their toil all the days God has given them under the sun."

Ecclesiastes is strikingly honest. It doesn't pretend life is easy—it admits it can be confusing, fleeting, and unfair. Yet right in the middle of those hard truths comes this gentle reminder: enjoy what God has given. Savor a meal. Laugh with friends. Find joy in the everyday moments, even in the middle of toil and struggle.

☆ MORE THAN A PARTY SLOGAN

"EAT, DRINK, AND BE MERRY" isn't just about indulgence. It's about learning to find joy in the everyday—not because everything is perfect, but because God is still good. It's about celebrating the simple gifts:

A good meal

A shared laugh

A quiet sunset

A hug from a friend

These aren't distractions from life—they're part of what makes it meaningful.

🪴 WHY IT MATTERS

Life can be overwhelming. Sometimes we feel guilty about enjoying ourselves, especially when things are hard or uncertain.

But the Bible reminds us: **Joy is not a luxury. It's a gift.**

God isn't just the God of sacrifice—He's also the God of celebration.

He wants us to laugh, feast, dance, and rejoice in the life He's given us.

Yes, life is temporary. But that doesn't make joy pointless.

It makes it **precious.**

THINK ABOUT IT

- What's something simple you've enjoyed lately—a moment, a meal, a conversation?

  _____
  _____
  _____
  _____
  _____

- How could celebrating that moment be an act of gratitude?

  _____
  _____
  _____
  _____
  _____

TRY THIS

Next time someone says, "EAT, DRINK, AND BE MERRY," you can say:

"That's from the Bible, actually! It's about enjoying the life God gives us— even when it's not perfect."

Joy might be the testimony someone didn't expect.

17

"FALL FROM GRACE"

(HOW DID I GET HERE? CAN I GO BACK?)

YOU MIGHT'VE HEARD SOMEONE SAY...

"FALLEN FROM GRACE"

Today, we say that when they lose respect, power, or trust—often after a mistake or scandal.

- A famous athlete caught cheating.
- A leader who lets pride lead to failure.
- A friend who breaks trust.

It's a phrase that can feel heavy... and it should, because its original meaning from the Bible is about losing something even greater than a good reputation—it's about losing touch with God's free gift of grace.

WHERE IT COMES FROM

The phrase comes from **Galatians 5:4,** where the apostle Paul writes:

> "You who are trying to be justified by the law have been alienated from Christ; you have fallen away from grace."

Paul was speaking to believers in Galatia who had started trusting religious rules to save them instead of trusting in Jesus. They were slipping back into thinking they could earn God's favor through performance, instead of living in the freedom of His gift.

Falling from grace in this context didn't mean losing salvation every time they stumbled—it meant turning away from the truth of the gospel and relying on their own effort.

⭐ FROM THE BIBLE TO EVERYDAY SPEECH

Over time, the phrase "fall from grace" came to mean any dramatic loss of honor or favor—whether spiritual or not.

It's used for public downfalls, career-ending mistakes, or moral failures. But at its root, it's about moving away from what was freely given—whether that's God's grace or the trust of others.

🪴 WHY IT MATTERS

God's grace is unearned.
We didn't climb up to get it—so why would we think we can keep it by climbing higher?

When we drift into thinking it's all on us, we stop resting in what Jesus has already done. That's when we risk "falling" into self-reliance, pride, or despair.

Grace isn't just how we start the Christian life—it's how we live it, every single day.

 **THINK ABOUT IT**

▸ Have you ever tried to earn someone's approval after you already had it?

▸ How can you rest in God's grace instead of striving for it?

🫱 TRY THIS

If someone says, "They've fallen from grace," you could say:

"That's actually from the Bible—it's about forgetting that we can't earn God's love, and losing sight of His grace."

It might be the reminder they (or you) need.

"FOR EVERYTHING, THERE IS A SEASON"

(BECAUSE WINTER DOESN'T LAST FOREVER)

YOU MIGHT'VE HEARD SOMEONE SAY...

"THIS IS JUST A SEASON."

People say it when life feels unsettled—after a breakup, during a job change, or while kids seem to grow up too fast. It's a soft reminder that change won't last forever.

But did you know this cliché comes straight from the Bible? It's actually part of one of the most poetic and well-loved passages ever written.

[?] WHERE IT COMES FROM

Ecclesiastes 3:1–8 says:

> "To everything there is a season, a time for every purpose under heaven..."

It goes on to name the ups and downs of life:

> "A time to be born, and a time to die... a time to weep, and a time to laugh... a time to mourn, and a time to dance..."

The writer isn't saying these seasons are always easy—but that they all have meaning. Even the painful ones. God, in His wisdom, allows every phase of life to shape us.

⭐ FROM THE RADIO TO REAL LIFE

Fun fact: this passage became a hit song in 1965 when The Byrds released "Turn! Turn! Turn!" using these exact words. That's how a 3,000-year-old Bible verse made it to the radio. But Ecclesiastes isn't just poetry set to music—it's making a point.

Every season of life has a purpose.

God doesn't waste joy or sorrow, beginnings or endings. The reminder is clear: instead of resisting change, we can recognize that each moment, light or heavy, is held in His hands.

🪴 WHY IT MATTERS

Seasons come and go, but God remains the same.

This verse reminds us that change is normal, even necessary. Hard moments won't last forever, and joyful ones are meant to be treasured.

Instead of fearing what's next, we can learn to ask: **"What is God doing in this season?"**

🧠 THINK ABOUT IT

- What kind of season are you in right now—one of growth, loss, waiting, or joy?

  _____
  _____
  _____
  _____
  _____

- How can you trust that God is at work even when life feels out of rhythm?

  _____
  _____
  _____
  _____
  _____

🫶 TRY THIS

If someone says, "IT'S JUST A SEASON," you could smile and say:

"That's from Ecclesiastes, actually. The Bible has this whole list of life seasons—it's kind of comforting knowing change is part of the plan."

19

"FIGHT THE GOOD FIGHT"
(GLOVES ON, HEART STEADY)

YOU MIGHT'VE HEARD SOMEONE SAY...

Maybe it was in a motivational speech.

Or from a coach before a big game.

Or from a friend when you were going through something tough:

"COME ON—FIGHT THE GOOD FIGHT!"

It's the kind of phrase that makes you want to stand a little taller and keep pushing forward.

But the original meaning? Way bigger than winning a trophy or passing a test.

[?] WHERE IT COMES FROM

The phrase comes straight from 1 Timothy 6:12:

> "Fight the good fight of the faith. Take hold of the eternal life to which you were called when you made your good confession in the presence of many witnesses."

Paul is writing to his protégé Timothy, reminding him that following Jesus isn't a spectator sport—it's an all-in commitment. The "fight" Paul is talking about isn't about fists or arguments; it's about standing firm in truth, living with integrity, and not giving up when things get hard.

⭐ MORE THAN JUST A PEP TALK

Paul knew life as a Christian can feel like a battleground. The challenges aren't just "out there" in the world—they're inside us too: doubts, fears, temptations, and weariness.

The "good fight" isn't about proving we're right; it's about holding onto what's true, even when it's unpopular or costly.

It's the daily decision to keep our faith alive and active—to keep loving, serving, forgiving, and trusting.

🌱 WHY IT MATTERS

Life will give you plenty of battles. Some are worth your time... others aren't. The "GOOD FIGHT" is the one worth giving your whole heart to—the fight to follow Jesus, to live with purpose, to love well, and to finish well.

It's about keeping your eyes on eternity, not just the struggle in front of you.

And here's the good news: *you don't fight alone.* God gives you His Spirit, His Word, and His people to strengthen you for every round.

THINK ABOUT IT

- What "fights" in your life are worth giving your time and energy to right now?

_____
_____
_____
_____

- What would it look like to approach those battles with God's strength instead of just your own?

_____
_____
_____
_____

TRY THIS

If someone says, "Fight the good fight," you could say:

"Yeah—that's actually from the Bible. Paul said it as a reminder to keep our faith strong, even when life gets tough. It's encouraging to think the fight is worth it because the goal is eternal life."

20
"FORBIDEN FRUIT"
(BUT IT'S JUST ONE BITE... RIGHT?)

YOU MIGHT'VE HEARD SOMEONE SAY...

"CAREFUL—THAT'S FORBIDDEN FRUIT."

Maybe in a romance movie when two people like each other but really shouldn't. Or when someone jokes about trying a risky, off-limits treat. It's that feeling where the thing you can't have suddenly feels irresistible.

But did you know this cliché comes from one of the oldest stories in the Bible?

🔖 WHERE IT COMES FROM

In Eden, God gave Adam and Eve everything they needed—plus one clear boundary:

> "But you must not eat from the tree of the knowledge of good and evil, for when you eat from it you will certainly die." (Genesis 2:17)

The fruit wasn't "bad" because of flavor; it was forbidden because eating it meant distrusting and disobeying God. Tempted by the serpent's lie, they took a bite—and that choice brought sin, brokenness, and death into the human story.

 MORE THAN JUST A BITE

We've been replaying that moment ever since—the shiny shortcut, the secret thrill, the "just this once" that snowballs. Adam and Eve lost more than a piece of fruit; they lost innocence, intimacy with God, and the peace they were made for.

And if we're honest, we know that feeling. We've all reached for what looked sweet, only to taste the bitterness later.

WHY IT MATTERS

Temptation rarely shows up waving red flags. It dresses itself in "No oNE WiLL KNoW" and "You DESERVE THIS." It convinces us that what God calls off-limits might actually be the best thing for us.

But every "FORBIDDEN FRUIT" comes with a cost—sometimes one we don't see until it's too late. God's boundaries aren't to hold us back, but to guard what's most precious. Trusting Him, even when the fruit looks good, is where real freedom begins.

🗨 THINK ABOUT IT

▶ What's a "forbidden fruit" you're tempted to taste right now?

_____
_____
_____
_____
_____

▶ How would trusting God in that moment protect something you value?

_____
_____
_____
_____
_____

🤚 TRY THIS

If someone jokes, "WELL.. IT'S FORBIDDEN FRUIT," you could say:

"That phrase is actually from the Bible—Eden stuff. It's a good reminder that not every shiny thing is good for us."

21
"GIVE UP THE GHOST"
(WHEN IT'S ALL OVER)

YOU MIGHT'VE HEARD SOMEONE SAY...

"IT FINALLY GAVE UP THE GHOST."

We say it when a computer crashes, a car won't start, or the office coffee maker gives out. Sometimes it's even used for a phone that won't charge no matter how many times you try.

But this phrase isn't just about worn-out machines—it's been around for centuries. Long before it landed in our everyday talk, it was used to describe people in the Bible, pointing to the moment life itself slips away.

❓ WHERE IT COMES FROM

The phrase shows up in the Bible in Genesis 25:8, describing the death of Abraham:

> "Then Abraham gave up the ghost, and died in a good old age, an old man, and full of years; and was gathered to his people."

It's an old way of saying someone's spirit or soul left their body—a poetic way to describe the moment of death. In Abraham's case, it paints a picture of a life well-lived, ending in peace.

⭐ MORE THAN JUST A PHRASE

Over time, "GIVE UP THE GHOST" drifted into everyday English as a way to talk about anything that stops working—often with a smirk. But in Scripture, it's about more than just something breaking down. It's about the sacred transition from this life to the next.

Abraham didn't "give up" in defeat; he completed his race, having lived long and faithfully.

🪴 WHY IT MATTERS

Death is one of those things we try not to think about—until we have to. But for those who belong to Jesus, "giving up the ghost" isn't the end of the story. It's the doorway into eternal life.

Abraham's peaceful passing reminds us that the goal isn't just to live long—it's to live well, so that when our time comes, we can face it with hope, not fear.

 THINK ABOUT IT

▶ If today were your last, what would you want to leave behind—memories, relationships, faith?

_____
_____
_____
_____
_____

▶ How would living with eternity in mind change your priorities now?

_____
_____
_____
_____
_____

TRY THIS

If someone says, "IT FINALLY GAVE UP THE GHOST," you could say:

"You know, that's actually a Bible phrase. It was first used about Abraham—he didn't just quit, he finished well."

22
"GO THE EXTRA MILE"
(MORE THAN WHAT'S ASKED)

YOU MIGHT'VE HEARD SOMEONE SAY...

"SHE REALLY WENT THE EXTRA MILE ON THIS PROJECT."

Maybe it was your boss thanking a coworker, or maybe a coach praises a player for giving it their all:

"THAT KID WENT THE EXTRA MILE FOR THE TEAM."

We use it to applaud **effort** that goes *above and beyond*. But the phrase? It started with Jesus.

[?] WHERE IT COMES FROM

In Matthew 5:41, Jesus told His followers:

> "If anyone forces you to go one mile, go with them two miles."

Back then, Roman soldiers could legally force civilians to carry their gear for one mile—a heavy, inconvenient task no one wanted. Jesus flips the script. Instead of grumbling through the mile, He tells His followers to surprise their oppressors by willingly walking a second one.

It wasn't just about carrying a load—it was about **carrying His love into unexpected places.**

⭐ MORE THAN JUST A PHRASE

It wasn't about mileage—it was about heart.

By going further than expected, Jesus' disciples showed love, humility, and a refusal to let bitterness rule their actions.

It turned a forced burden into a chosen act of service. And that kind of choice? It still stands out today.

🪴 WHY IT MATTERS

Life gives us "one-mile" moments all the time—tasks, interruptions, or people who drain us. The easy route is to do the bare minimum.

But Jesus calls us higher.

Going the extra mile isn't just about effort—it's about love that refuses to keep score, service that doesn't demand applause, and generosity that reflects God's heart.

When we go beyond what's required, we shine a little more of Him into ordinary moments.

🗣 THINK ABOUT IT

▶ What's an area of your life where you've been tempted to only do the bare minimum?

_____
_____
_____
_____
_____

▶ How could "going the extra mile" change the way others see Jesus in you?

_____
_____
_____
_____
_____

🤲 TRY THIS

If someone says, "THANKS FOR GOING THE EXTRA MILE," you could reply:

"Did you know Jesus was actually the first to say that? He used it to show that love goes beyond what's expected."

23
"HEART OF STONE"
COLDER THAN A FREEZER BURN

YOU MIGHT'VE HEARD SOMEONE SAY...

"HE'S GOT A HEART OF STONE."

It's one of those phrases people use when describing someone who seems *cold, detached, or unmoved* by anything. Over time, it's become shorthand for **emotional rigidity**—an unwillingness to show empathy, compassion, or kindness.

Maybe you've heard it about a boss who didn't care about his employees, a politician ignoring the hurting, or that kid at school who seemed immune to kindness. Whatever the case, the picture is the same: **someone who just doesn't care.**

❓ WHERE IT COMES FROM

In Ezekiel 36:26, God makes a promise to His people:

> "I will give you a new heart and put a new spirit in you; I will remove from you your heart of stone and give you a heart of flesh."

A "HEART OF STONE" symbolized stubbornness, rebellion, and *spiritual deadness*—an unresponsive life that **refused to love God** or others. But God didn't just diagnose the problem; *He gave the cure*. He promised to replace that stone with a living, beating heart filled with His Spirit.

 MORE THAN JUST A METAPHOR

This wasn't about better manners or a self-help upgrade. It was about transformation.

God wasn't asking His people to chip away at *their own hardness*—He promised to perform a heart transplant.

The very things we can't change in ourselves? He can.

 WHY IT MATTERS

We all know what it's like to *grow cold*. Maybe **disappointment** hardened you. Maybe **sin** calloused you.

Maybe **hurt** made you shut down.

But God doesn't leave us stuck. He can soften what's become rigid, heal what's been scarred, and make us tender again—toward Him and toward people. A heart that beats with His love *changes* how we live, forgive, and serve.

🗨️ THINK ABOUT IT

▶ Have you noticed any "hard spots" in your heart—areas where you've grown cold or resistant to God

_____
_____
_____
_____

▶ What would it look like for God to soften those areas and fill them with His Spirit?

_____
_____
_____
_____

🫶 TRY THIS

If someone says, "HE'S GOT A HEART OF STONE,"
you could say:

"You know? the Bible actually uses that picture too—but it also promises that God can give us a brand-new heart."

 "THE HANDWRITING ON THE WALL"

(WHEN THE SIGNS COULDN'T BE CLEARER)

YOU MIGHT'VE HEARD SOMEONE SAY...

"LOOKS LIKE THE HANDWRITING'S ON THE WALL."

People say it when trouble is obviously coming—a company about to go bankrupt, a sports team losing badly, or a relationship on its last legs. It's another way of saying, *"The end is near, and you can't ignore*

WHERE IT COMES FROM

The phrase goes all the way back to the book of Daniel. King Belshazzar of Babylon threw a wild banquet, drinking from the sacred cups stolen from God's temple. In the middle of the party, a mysterious hand appeared and wrote a cryptic message on the palace wall:

"MENE, MENE, TEKEL, PARSIN." (Daniel 5:5, 25).

No one could read it—until Daniel explained that it meant Belshazzar's kingdom had been judged and would soon fall. That very night, Babylon was conquered.

⭐ BEFORE IT'S TOO LATE

The handwriting on the wall wasn't just a creepy miracle. It was God giving Belshazzar one last warning before judgment fell. Ignoring it didn't make it go away—it only sealed his fate.

We might not get glowing letters on plaster today, but God still gives warnings—through Scripture, through conscience, even through people who care enough to speak truth. The question is: do we listen, or do we keep partying like nothing's wrong?

🪴 WHY IT MATTERS

None of us like warnings—they feel uncomfortable. But warnings are actually mercy. They mean there's still time to change course.

Whether it's the "HANDWRITING ON THE WALL" in your own choices or the gentle nudge of conviction, God's call to turn around isn't meant to shame you—it's meant to save you.

🧠 THINK ABOUT IT

▶ Have you ever ignored a warning and regretted it later?

_____
_____
_____
_____
_____

▶ What "handwriting on the wall" might God be showing you right now?

_____
_____
_____
_____
_____

🤲 TRY THIS

If someone says, "WELL, THE HANDWRITING'S ON THE WALL," you could respond:

"That's a pretty strange phrase. Do you know where it comes from? It's actually from the Bible—God was literally warning a king. Makes me think how He still gives us signs before things go bad."

"HOW THE MIGHTY HAVE FALLEN"

(WHEN HEROES HIT THE GROUND)

YOU MIGHT'VE HEARD SOMEONE SAY...

WOW... HOW THE MIGHTY HAVE FALLEN."

It's the go-to phrase when a celebrity crashes from fame, a politician gets caught in scandal, or a sports dynasty suddenly tanks after years of winning. It captures that mix of shock and irony when someone at the top comes tumbling down.

[?] WHERE IT COMES FROM

The line comes from one of the most moving laments in the Bible. In 2 Samuel 1:19–25, David hears the news that Saul and Jonathan have been killed in battle. You might expect relief—Saul had hunted him for years—but instead David broke down in grief.

His song repeats the words three times: "How the mighty have fallen." Each repetition carries the weight of loss—shock, sorrow, and the ache of finality.

David remembered them not for their flaws but for their courage, strength, and glory. His words remind us that even the strongest can fall, leaving a wound on all who loved them.

 NOT A PUNCHLINE

Today we usually use the phrase with a smirk—when a celebrity stumbles, a team loses, or a company fails. But in Scripture, it carried a deep sadness.

David wasn't mocking Saul and Jonathan; he was mourning the loss of leaders who once carried the hopes of Israel.

His words remind us that even the strongest among us are fragile, that greatness without God quickly fades, and that every fall leaves behind real grief for those left standing.

WHY IT MATTERS

We live in a world that loves to watch people rise—and even more to watch them fall. But David's response reminds us to see with compassion, not mockery. When others stumble, our first reaction shouldn't be pride or gossip, but grief and humility. Their fall is a warning to us, too: without God, no strength or success can stand. True greatness isn't about staying on top—it's about staying close to Him.

🗣 THINK ABOUT IT

- How do you usually respond when you see someone "fall from greatness"—with judgment, or with compassion?

  _____
  _____
  _____
  _____
  _____

- What does your reaction reveal about where your own security is rooted?

  _____
  _____
  _____
  _____
  _____

🫶 TRY THIS

If someone says, "Wow, how the mighty have fallen," you could respond:

"Yeah, that phrase is actually from the Bible. David said it when he was grieving over fallen leaders—not mocking them. It makes me think how easy it is for any of us to fall without God's strength."

One moment of truth... one open door.

26
"IN THE TWINKLING OF AN EYE"
(WHEN TIME IS AGAINST US)

YOU MIGHT'VE HEARD SOMEONE SAY...

"IT HAPPENED IN THE TWINKLING OF AN EYE."

People say it when something happens really fast—like when your snack disappears, your favorite show ends before you realize it, or a weekend flies by in what feels like seconds. It's a fun way to describe how quickly things can change. One moment everything's calm, and the next—boom!—it's different. It reminds us how fast life moves, and how quickly everything around us can shift.

⍰ WHERE IT COMES FROM

This phrase actually comes from the Bible (1 Corinthians 15:52). Paul wrote:

> "In a flash, in the twinkling of an eye, at the last trumpet. For the trumpet will sound, the dead will be raised imperishable, and we will be changed."

He was talking about the day Jesus comes back. Paul said that in a single blink—so fast you can't even time it—everything will change. No more sickness, no more death, no more sadness. Just like that.

⭐ MORE THAN A BLINK

People today this phrase to talk about speed, but Paul was pointing to hope.

The point isn't just "wow, THAT'S FAST"—it's that when God moves, He can turn everything around in an instant. One moment, life can feel heavy and broken, and in the next, He can make it whole again.

🌱 WHY IT MATTERS

We all have moments that feel like they'll never end—tough days, big losses, waiting for answers. But this phrase reminds us that God's rescue comes quickly, and His promises are sure.

Even when it feels slow to us, He hasn't forgotten. And one day, He'll fix everything in the blink of an eye.

🧠 THINK ABOUT IT

▶ What's something in your life that feels like it's taking forever?

_____
_____
_____
_____

▶ How does it help you to know that God can change things faster than we can even imagine?

_____
_____
_____
_____

🤲 TRY THIS

Next time someone says, "IT HAPPENED IN THE BLINK OF AN EYE," you could smile and say:

"Did you know the Bible uses that phrase? It's about how fast God can change everything when Jesus comes back."

27
"IN THE BEGINNING"
(EVERY STORY STARTS SOMEWHERE)

YOU MIGHT'VE HEARD SOMEONE SAY...

"IN THE BEGINNING..."

It's how stories often start. Fairytales open with it, movies hint at it, even grandparents use it to kick off a long tale. It signals, this is where everything started.

But the Bible used it first—not as a bedtime story, but as the most important introduction ever written. Instead of "once upon a time," it begins with God, setting the stage for everything else.

[?] WHERE IT COMES FROM

Genesis 1:1 says:

> "In the beginning, God created the heavens and the earth."

These opening words don't just mark time, they declare the Author. Before galaxies swirled or waves crashed, God already was. He spoke, and the universe leapt into being—light, land, oceans, creatures, us. This isn't random chance; it's intentional creation, born out of God's design and power.

⭐ MORE THAN JUST AN OPENING LINE

When we say "IN THE BEGINNING," we just mean the start of something.

But Genesis uses it to tell us who the beginning belongs to. God is not just part of the story—He is the beginning. Every sunrise, every heartbeat, every new chapter in history and in your life begins with Him.

That's why the Bible's very first words are so weighty—they're not just marking a start, **they're pointing us back to the One who started it all.**

🪴 WHY IT MATTERS

Starting over isn't always easy. First days at school, moving into a new place, changing jobs, or stepping into the unknown can make us nervous.

Genesis reminds us that no beginning is outside of God's reach. The same God who spoke light into darkness is the One guiding you into each new chapter.

When life feels uncertain, remember this: every beginning belongs to Him—and with Him, there's always hope.

🗣 THINK ABOUT IT

- What "new beginning" are you facing right now?

  _____
  _____
  _____
  _____

- How does remembering God was there "in the beginning" give you confidence today?

  _____
  _____
  _____
  _____

🤲 TRY THIS

When someone says, "WELL, IN THE BEGINNING..." you could grin and reply:

"Did you know that's how the Bible starts? It's a cool reminder that God was there before everything—and He's still here now."

28

"LOVE THY NEIGHBOR AS THYSELF"

NOT A SMALL THING TO ASK

YOU MIGHT'VE HEARD SOMEONE SAY...

"LOVE YOUR NEIGHBOR AS YOURSELF."

It sounds like something you'd see on a bumper sticker or hear in a classroom kindness talk. It's one of the most famous sayings about being nice.

But here's the thing: long before it was a slogan, it was a command. And it's not about fuzzy feelings—it's about **real action**: helping, forgiving, showing compassion. Treating others the way you'd want to be treated.

This little phrase is more than a cliché. It's the heartbeat of God's law.

WHERE IT COMES FROM

This phrase first shows up in Leviticus 19:18:

> "Do not seek revenge or bear a grudge against anyone among your people, but love your neighbor as yourself. I am the Lord."

God wasn't giving Israel a suggestion—He was laying down the heartbeat of His law. To love your neighbor meant forgiving instead of getting even, helping instead of ignoring, showing compassion instead of holding grudges.

⭐ MORE THAN GOOD ADVICE

Today, "LOVE YOUR NEIGHBOR" often gets watered down into a feel-good slogan. But in Scripture, it's weighty. Jesus even said this command, alongside loving God, sums up the whole Law and Prophets (Matthew 22:37–40).

That means if you miss this, you miss the point.

🪴 WHY IT MATTERS

If everyone loved like this, grudges would die quickly, families would heal faster, and communities would grow stronger and safer.

Imagine a world where forgiveness was normal, kindness was expected, and no one felt alone. But the truth is—we struggle even with the basics. We get selfish. We hold onto hurts. We find it easier to judge than to show grace.

That's why this phrase points us beyond ourselves: **only when God's love fills us, renews us, and softens our hearts can we truly love others in the same way He loves us.**

🗣 THINK ABOUT IT

▶ Who in your life is hardest for you to love right now?

_____
_____
_____
_____
_____

▶ Do you treat yourself with kindness and grace—or are you harsh even with yourself? How might that affect how you treat others?

_____
_____
_____
_____
_____

🫱 TRY THIS

If someone says, "LOVE YOUR NEIGHBOR AS YOURSELF," you could smile and say:

"True—and it makes me think, we can't really love people that way unless we first know God's love ourselves."

"MANY ARE CALLED, BUT FEW ARE CHOSEN"

(WHEN INVITES AREN'T ENOUGH)

YOU MIGHT'VE HEARD SOMEONE SAY...

"MANY ARE CALLED, BUT FEW ARE CHOSEN."

It's a phrase people throw around when only a handful make the cut—whether it's the sports team, a scholarship, or a talent show. Most hear the call, but only a few walk away with the prize. It sounds discouraging, almost unfair.

But Jesus wasn't talking about auditions or tryouts—He was revealing something deeper about God's kingdom.

❓ WHERE IT COMES FROM

The line comes from one of Jesus' parables about the kingdom of heaven. In Matthew 22, He tells the story of a king who prepared a wedding feast for his son. Invitations went out to many, but most guests refused to come. Some ignored it, others mistreated the messengers. So the king opened the doors wide and invited anyone willing to come. Yet when the feast began, one man entered without proper wedding clothes and was cast out.

At the end, Jesus summed it up with this striking line: **"For many are called, but few are chosen"** (Matthew 22:14).

⭐ THE DIFFERENCE IS IN THE YES

Jesus' words weren't about exclusivity, as if God only handpicks a secret few. Instead, He highlighted the difference between hearing an invitation and truly responding to it.

Many hear the gospel, but not all accept it. Some shrug it off, others get distracted, and some want the benefits of the feast without honoring the King.

Being "chosen" isn't about God playing favorites—it's about who humbles themselves to receive His grace.

The chosen are the ones who come on His terms, not their own.

🪴 WHY IT MATTERS

This phrase reminds us that faith is more than proximity. Sitting in church, hearing sermons, or even knowing Bible verses doesn't make us part of God's family. What matters is saying "yes" to His Son and letting that choice reshape our lives.

The call of God goes out to all people—no one is excluded from the invitation. But entering His kingdom requires a response, a surrender. The "chosen" aren't the best or the brightest—they're the forgiven who trusted the King's mercy.

 THINK ABOUT IT

▶ How do you usually respond when God nudges your heart—do you delay, ignore, or accept?

_____
_____
_____
_____ v
_____

▶ What's one area of your life where you've heard His call but haven't yet acted on it?

_____
_____
_____
_____
_____

🫴 TRY THIS

If someone says, "WELL, MANY ARE CALLED, BUT FEW ARE CHOSEN," you could reply:

"Yeah, Jesus said that—but it wasn't about some elite club. He was talking about God's invitation. The amazing thing is, we're all invited to His feast. The real question is: will we say yes to Him?"

"NO REST FOR THE WICKED"

(WAIT... WHO NEEDS REST ANYWAY?)

YOU MIGHT'VE HEARD SOMEONE SAY...

"WELL, NO REST FOR THE WICKED!"

It usually comes up when life is busy—like a coworker joking about staying late, a parent juggling errands, or even in music lyrics.

It's said with a grin, but it carries a serious undertone: If you're in the thick of it, don't expect a break.

Funny thing is, the phrase didn't start out as a comment about busyness— it's actually a warning straight from God.

❓ WHERE IT COMES FROM

The phrase comes from Isaiah 48:22, where God declares:

"There is no peace," says the Lord, "for the wicked."

The prophet Isaiah was delivering God's message to people who had turned away from Him. They thought they could ignore His commands and still be fine—but God made it clear: a life of rebellion leads to unrest.

The kind of "no rest" He's talking about isn't just physical exhaustion—it's the deep lack of peace that comes from running from God.

⭐ MORE THAN JUST A JOKE

These days, "no rest for the wicked" is tossed around like an excuse for being busy. But in Scripture, it's much more serious. Sin eats away at peace. Wickedness isn't just doing something "really bad"—it's living as if God doesn't matter. And when we try to carry life on our own terms, the result isn't rest but weariness.

Here's the good news: Jesus came to give true rest. He said, "Come to Me, all who are weary and burdened, and I will give you rest" *(Matt. 11:28)*. The contrast is clear: life apart from God brings turmoil; life with Him brings peace.

🪴 WHY IT MATTERS

We live in a restless world. Stress, anxiety, and endless striving are everywhere. Sometimes we try to laugh it off with a cliché—but the truth is, deep down, we all crave peace.

The promise of the gospel is that rest isn't found in doing more, earning more, or hiding our brokenness. It's found in Jesus. He takes the weight of sin, the guilt, the constant running—and replaces it with His peace.

🗣 THINK ABOUT IT

▶ Where do you notice restlessness in your own life—your thoughts, habits, or relationships?

_____
_____
_____
_____

▶ What would it look like to trade that for the kind of peace only Jesus gives?

_____
_____
_____
_____

🫶 TRY THIS

Next time someone sighs, "NO REST FOR THE WICKED," you can reply:

"Funny enough, that comes from the Bible—it's about how real peace comes only from God."

Who knows? That little comment might turn a tired joke into an open door for hope.

31
"OUT OF THE MOUTHS OF BABES"

(CAN KIDS REALLY TEACH US SOMETHING?)

YOU MIGHT'VE HEARD SOMEONE SAY...

"OUT OF THE MOUTHS OF BABES!"

Usually it's after a child blurts out something surprisingly sharp, funny, or even profound. Kids have a way of saying what's on everyone's mind—or cutting through the noise with a simple truth adults might miss.

It's a phrase we toss around lightheartedly, but it actually comes from one of the most beautiful psalms in the Bible.

❓ WHERE IT COMES FROM

The phrase comes from Psalm 8:2: }

> "Through the praise of children and infants you have established a stronghold against your enemies, to silence the foe and the avenger."

David, the psalmist, is marveling at God's glory in creation. And right in the middle of it, he notes that God uses the praise of little ones to show His strength.

In other words, the words of children—weak and dependent as they seem—can silence the enemy. God delights in working through what looks small to the world.

☆ MORE THAN JUST A JOKE

We often think wisdom comes only from the experienced, the educated, or the eloquent.

But God flips that upside down.

Sometimes He chooses the least expected voices—like kids—to remind us of truth. Their honesty, their praise, even their questions can humble us and point us back to God.

That's what makes this phrase more than just a laugh-worthy moment: it's a reminder that God can use anyone, at any age, to show His greatness.

🪴 WHY IT MATTERS

We live in a world where loud voices often get the attention. But God reminds us that He values humility, sincerity, and dependence on Him—qualities we often see most clearly in children.

Their faith, unfiltered words, and simple praise can teach us more than we realize. Jesus Himself said we should receive the kingdom of God like a child. Maybe that's because kids remind us that faith isn't about being impressive—it's about being honest and trusting.

🗨️ THINK ABOUT IT

- When's the last time a child surprised you with their honesty or insight?

  _____
  _____
  _____
  _____

- What could you learn from a childlike faith in your own walk with God?

  _____
  _____
  _____
  _____

🤲 TRY THIS

Next time someone says, "OUT OF THE MOUTHS OF BABES," you can say:

"That phrase is actually from the Psalms—God uses even children's words and praise to show His power."

A simple reminder that God often speaks through the smallest voices.

32

"PRIDE COMES BEFORE A FALL"

(OOPS... DIDN'T SEE THAT COMING)

YOU MIGHT'VE HEARD SOMEONE SAY...

"PRIDE COMES BEFORE A FALL."

It's often dropped like a wise proverb when someone's acting a little too confident—or right after they've been proven wrong.

Think of the athlete boasting before a game, the student sure they don't need to study, or the driver bragging they never get lost... only to take the wrong exit.

It's funny in the moment, but the phrase actually comes from a sobering truth in Scripture.

❓ WHERE IT COMES FROM

The saying originates in Proverbs 16:18:

> "Pride goes before destruction, a haughty spirit before a fall."

The wisdom here is straightforward: **pride makes us blind.** It puffs us up and convinces us we don't need God—or anyone else. But that kind of arrogance sets us up for a crash.

The book of Proverbs is full of warnings like this, reminding us that *humility leads to life*, while pride leads to ruin.

⭐ THE REAL DANGER OF PRIDE

In everyday use, the phrase can feel like a punchline. But biblically, it's a serious diagnosis.

Pride isn't just bragging—it's putting ourselves at the center instead of God. And when we live that way, we stumble.

Pride whispers, "You've got this. You're enough." But Scripture reminds us: the moment we believe that lie, we're already slipping.

Humility, on the other hand, opens the door for God's grace and strength.

🪴 WHY IT MATTERS

We all wrestle with pride. Sometimes it's obvious, sometimes it hides in our hearts as self-reliance, comparison, or resistance to correction. But the gospel shows us another way.

Jesus humbled Himself—even to the cross. And because of that humility, He was lifted up.

Our call is the same: to walk humbly, to depend on God, and to remember that the way up always begins by bowing down.

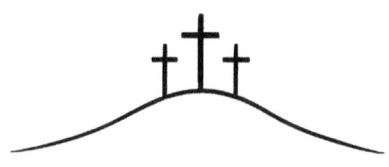

 THINK ABOUT IT

▶ Where do you notice pride creeping into your own thoughts or actions?

_____
_____
_____
_____

▶ What would it look like to choose humility in that area instead?

_____
_____
_____
_____

TRY THIS

Next time someone says, "PRIDE COMES BEFORE A FALL," you can say:

"That's straight from Proverbs—it's a reminder that humility keeps us standing firm, but pride always makes us stumble."

A little phrase with a big truth behind it.

33

"RISE AND SHINE"

(TIME TO WAKE UP!)

YOU MIGHT'VE HEARD SOMEONE SAY...

"RISE AND SHINE!"

Maybe it was your mom flipping on the lights in the morning, a coach trying to pump up the team, or even a cheery voice on the radio.

These days, it's mostly a playful way to say, "Get up and get moving!" But the original phrase isn't just about mornings—it's about something much bigger.

❓ WHERE IT COMES FROM

The idea comes from Isaiah 60:1:

> "Arise, shine, for your light has come, and the glory of the Lord rises upon you."

Isaiah was speaking to God's people, who had been through seasons of exile and discouragement.

His message was simple but powerful: God's light has come—so get up and let it shine on you.

This wasn't about dragging yourself out of bed—it was about waking up spiritually, stepping out of darkness, and walking in God's glory.

⭐ MORE THAN A MORNING PEP TALK

"RISE AND SHINE" in everyday language is lighthearted. But in Scripture, it's an invitation. God's light doesn't just brighten our morning—**it transforms our lives.**

When His glory shines on us, we're called to reflect it, like mirrors catching the sun.

The world doesn't need more sleepy faith—it needs people who are awake to God's goodness, living in His light, and letting that light shine through them.

🪴 WHY IT MATTERS

We all know what it's like to feel stuck, tired, or spiritually sluggish. But God's call is the same today as it was through Isaiah: **Arise.** Not in your own strength, but because His light has already come. Jesus said, "I am the light of the world." And when we follow Him, even the darkest places in our hearts and lives begin to glow with His hope.

That's the kind of "RISE AND SHINE" we all need.

 **THINK ABOUT IT**

▶ Where in your life do you feel like you're still in the dark or half-asleep spiritually?

_____
_____
_____
_____

▶ What would it look like to let God's light shine on you today?

_____
_____
_____
_____

🫴 TRY THIS

Next time someone chirps, "RISE AND SHINE!" you can reply:

"Did you know that's inspired by Isaiah? It's really about letting God's light wake us up and shine through us."

A playful phrase with a powerful promise.

34
"SCAPEGOAT"
(SOMEBODY HAS TO TAKE THE BLAME... RIGHT?)

YOU MIGHT'VE HEARD SOMEONE SAY...

"WELL, I GUESS I'M THE SCAPEGOAT."

It's what people say when they're unfairly blamed for something—like the employee who takes the fall for the boss's mistake, or the sibling who gets grounded when "technically" it wasn't their idea.

In everyday talk, it's all about dodging responsibility by pinning it on someone else.

But the term didn't start in an office or a family feud—it started in one of the most solemn rituals in the Old Testament.

WHERE IT COMES FROM

The term comes from Leviticus 16:8–10, in the instructions for the Day of Atonement (Yom Kippur). The high priest, Aaron, would cast lots over two goats:

- One goat was sacrificed as a sin offering.
- The other—the scapegoat—was symbolically loaded with the sins of the people and sent into the wilderness, carrying their guilt away.

This powerful picture showed that sin brings guilt, but God makes a way for it to be removed. The scapegoat wasn't just "taking the blame"—it represented the hope of being cleansed and set free.

⭐ MORE THAN A FALL GUY

Today, calling someone a SCAPEGOAT usually feels unfair. But in Scripture, the scapegoat was *God's merciful provision*. It pointed forward to something greater:

Jesus Himself. On the cross, He became the true and final scapegoat, taking our sins upon Himself and carrying them away—once and for all. What people now use as a cliché was originally a prophecy of the gospel.

🪴 WHY IT MATTERS

We all know what it feels like to want to shift the blame—or to be crushed under guilt that isn't ours. But the good news is, we **don't have to carry sin ourselves.** Jesus already bore it. Unlike the scapegoat that wandered into the wilderness year after year, He took our guilt permanently. That means we can stop running, stop hiding, and start living free—because our sins are gone.

🔊 THINK ABOUT IT

▶ Have you ever been someone else's "scapegoat"—blamed for what wasn't yours?

_____
_____
_____
_____
_____

▶ How does it change things to know Jesus willingly became your scapegoat?

_____
_____
_____
_____
_____
_____

🫶 TRY THIS

Next time someone says, "I'M JUST THE SCAPEGOAT," you can say:

> "You know, that word comes from the Bible. It was a picture of how God removes sin—and it points straight to Jesus."

A cliché with roots in the most powerful exchange of all time.

"SEEK AND YOU SHALL FIND"

(LOST KEYS... OR SOMETHING BIGGER?)

YOU MIGHT'VE HEARD SOMEONE SAY...

"WELL, SEEK AND YOU SHALL FIND!"

Maybe it was about car keys, missing socks, or even the perfect vacation spot online. It's usually tossed around as a way of saying, *"If you look hard enough, you'll get it."*

But before it became a cliché about everyday searching, it was one of Jesus' most comforting promises.

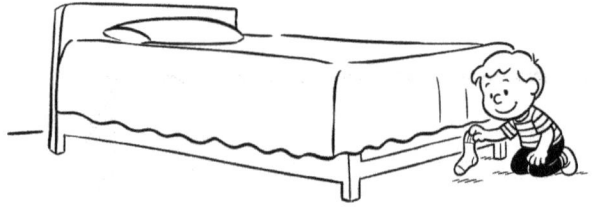

[?] WHERE IT COMES FROM

The phrase comes from Matthew 7:7, where Jesus says:

> "Ask, and it will be given to you; seek, and you will find; knock, and the door will be opened to you."

Jesus wasn't giving a tip for lost-and-found items. He was teaching about prayer—inviting His followers to come boldly to God.

Asking, seeking, and knocking weren't just actions; they were pictures of persistence, faith, and trust that God is listening and ready to answer.

☆ MORE THAN A MOTIVATIONAL QUOTE

Today, we use this phrase to talk about determination: **keep trying** until you succeed. That's not wrong, but Jesus was pointing to *something deeper*.

Seeking God isn't about demanding what we want—it's about discovering who He is.

When we seek Him, we don't just find answers, we find Him. And that's the greatest discovery of all.

🪴 WHY IT MATTERS

Life is full of searching—searching for purpose, direction, peace, or hope.

Some searches leave us empty, but Jesus' promise still stands: if you seek God with your whole heart, you will find Him.

Not because we're so good at looking, but because He delights to be found. And when we do, we discover the *one thing* we can never lose: **His presence.**

THINK ABOUT IT

▶ What's something you've been "seeking" lately—peace, answers, guidance?

_____
_____
_____
_____
_____

▶ How would your search look different if you sought God first?

_____
_____
_____
_____
_____

TRY THIS

Next time someone shrugs and says, "SEEK AND YOU SHALL FIND," you can reply:

"Jesus said that—He was inviting people to seek Him, and they'd discover so much more than they expected."

A familiar phrase with a far deeper treasure behind it.

"THE BLIND LEADING THE BLIND"

(WHO'S REALLY SHOWING THE WAY?)

YOU MIGHT'VE HEARD SOMEONE SAY...

"WELL, THAT'S JUST THE BLIND LEADING THE BLIND."

It's usually said when clueless people are trying to help each other out—like one student tutoring another who didn't do the homework, or a rookie showing a fellow rookie how to use the new software. It's funny in everyday use, but Jesus first used this phrase as a serious warning.

❓ WHERE IT COMES FROM

The phrase comes from Matthew 15:14, where Jesus says:

> "Leave them; they are blind guides. If the blind lead the blind, both will fall into a pit."

He was speaking about religious leaders who looked impressive on the outside but had no real understanding of God's truth.

They were teaching *traditions* instead of God's Word, and Jesus wanted His disciples to see the danger. His point? **If you follow someone who doesn't know where they're going spiritually, you'll both end up lost.**

⭐ MORE THAN JUST INCOMPETENCE

Today, the phrase "THE BLIND LEADING THE BLIND" is often used as a joke—when someone clueless tries to guide someone just as lost. But when Jesus said it, He wasn't talking about ignorance; He was warning about spiritual blindness.

The religious leaders claimed to know the truth but were walking in darkness, leading others there too. The real danger isn't being uninformed; it's refusing to let God correct our vision.

When pride or tradition keep us from His light, we stumble and cause others to do the same. But when we follow Jesus—the true Light of the world—our steps become sure, and we can help others find their way.

🪴 WHY IT MATTERS

We all follow someone. The question is:

Are they leading us closer to God or further from Him?

The world is full of "guides" offering wisdom, success, and spirituality—but not every voice points to truth. Jesus is the one guide who doesn't just see the path—**He is the path.** Following Him means we won't end up in the pit, but in the light of life.

🗣 THINK ABOUT IT

- Who are the "guides" you're listening to most—friends, media, influencers?

  _____
  _____
  _____
  _____
  _____

- How can you make sure the voices shaping you are pointing you toward Jesus?

  _____
  _____
  _____
  _____
  _____

🫶 TRY THIS

Next time someone says, "THAT'S THE BLIND LEADING THE BLIND," you can say:

> "Jesus actually used that phrase—He said we all need the right guide, and He's the one who never leads us wrong."

A phrase that starts with confusion...
but points to clarity in Christ.

"THE POWERS THAT BE"

(WHO PUT THEM IN CHARGE ANYWAY?)

YOU MIGHT'VE HEARD SOMEONE SAY...

"WELL, THE POWERS THAT BE DECIDED..."

Usually it's said with a shrug and maybe a mutter, when some boss, official, or committee makes a call that affects everyone else. It's become a shorthand way of talking about whoever's *"in charge,"* whether in politics, school, or the workplace.

But before it became an everyday cliché, it was Paul who first used the phrase to describe something much bigger.

WHERE IT COMES FROM

The phrase comes from Romans 13:1, where Paul writes:

> "Let everyone be subject to the governing authorities, for there is no authority except that which God has established. The authorities that exist have been established by God."

Paul was writing to Christians in Rome, reminding them that even imperfect governments and leaders fall under God's ultimate authority. His point wasn't that rulers are flawless or that injustice should be ignored—it was that behind all human power stands the greater power of God.

⭐ MORE THAN RED TAPE

Today, "THE POWERS THAT BE" can sound cynical, like we're at the mercy of distant decision-makers.

But Scripture reminds us that God is never distant. He allows authority for the sake of order, justice, and protection.

And when human leaders fail, we can still trust that God is sovereign. The powers that be aren't ultimate—*He is*.

🪴 WHY IT MATTERS

Authority can be frustrating, even unfair. But Romans 13 calls us to a posture of humility and trust. Respecting leaders doesn't mean blind obedience—it means recognizing God's hand in history, praying for those in authority, and living honorably under Him. And when we feel powerless, it reminds us that the true King is still on the throne.

🎧 THINK ABOUT IT

▸ How do you usually feel when "THE POWERS THAT BE" make decisions that affect you?

_____
_____
_____
_____

▸ What would change if you trusted that God is above every earthly authority?

_____
_____
_____
_____

🤝 TRY THIS

Next time someone says, "Well, the powers that be decided," you can respond:

"Funny enough, that phrase comes from the Bible—it reminds us that no authority is higher than God's."

A phrase about power... that points us to the ultimate authority.

"THE ROOT OF ALL EVIL"

(IS MONEY REALLY THE PROBLEM?)

YOU MIGHT'VE HEARD SOMEONE SAY...

"MONEY IS THE ROOT OF ALL EVIL."

It pops up in movies, political debates, or even casual conversations about greed. It sounds like the Bible is blaming money itself for everything wrong in the world. But the actual verse says something a little different—and a lot more revealing.

❓ WHERE IT COMES FROM

The phrase comes from 1 Timothy 6:10:

"For the love of money is a root of all kinds of evil."

Notice the difference? It's not money itself that's the root—it's the love of money. Paul was warning young Timothy about people who were so obsessed with wealth that it led them into harmful desires and even pulled them away from the faith. The issue wasn't having money; it was letting money have them.

☆ WHEN ENOUGH IS NEVER ENOUGH

Over time, "money is the root of all evil" became a cultural shorthand. But Scripture's message is deeper.

Money is a tool—it can provide, bless, and build. But when it becomes the thing we chase above God, it becomes a trap.

Love of money whispers, *"You need more. You'll never have enough."* And that chase leaves us empty. Jesus Himself said, "You cannot serve both God and money."

🌱 WHY IT MATTERS

We all wrestle with the pull of money, whether it's craving more or fearing not enough. The gospel reminds us that true security doesn't come from wealth but from Christ. When our hearts are set on Him, money stops being a master and starts being a servant—a resource to love others, serve God, and do good.

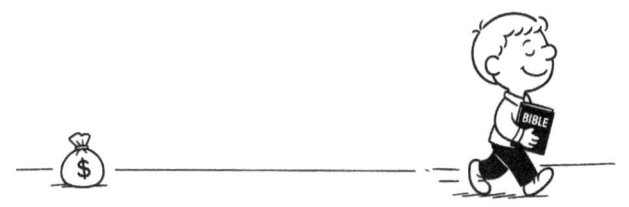

🗣 THINK ABOUT IT

- Where does money tug on your heart the most—desire, fear, or comparison?

  _____
  _____
  _____
  _____
  _____

- How might you use what you have as a tool for God's purposes instead of a source of worry or pride?

  _____
  _____
  _____
  _____
  _____

🤲 TRY THIS

Next time someone says, "WELL, MONEY IS THE ROOT OF ALL EVIL," you can say:

"Actually, the Bible says it's the love of money—that's what gets us in trouble. Money itself can be used for good."

A cliché about money... that points us back to what really matters.

 "THE SALT OF THE EARTH"
(A LITTLE FLAVOR GOES A LONG WAY)

YOU MIGHT'VE HEARD SOMEONE SAY...

"THE SALT OF THE EARTH."

It's usually said as a big compliment—about that humble neighbor who helps everyone, the coworker who never complains, or the friend who's just steady and kind. It paints a picture of someone genuine, grounded, and good. But when Jesus first used this phrase, He was describing more than personality—He was describing purpose.

❓ WHERE IT COMES FROM

The phrase comes from Matthew 5:13, where Jesus tells His followers:

> "You are the salt of the earth. But if the salt loses its saltiness, how can it be made salty again? It is no longer good for anything, except to be thrown out and trampled underfoot."

Salt in the ancient world wasn't just seasoning—it was vital. It preserved food, added flavor, and symbolized purity. Jesus was telling His disciples: Your presence matters. Just like salt changes what it touches, His followers were meant to make a difference in the world around them.

⭐ GOODNESS THAT CHANGES THINGS

Today, calling someone "SALT OF THE EARTH" is about being decent and dependable. But Jesus was inviting His disciples into something much bigger: living lives that preserve truth, bring out the goodness in others, and keep the world from decaying under sin. Being "salty" in His sense isn't about attitude—it's about impact.

🪴 WHY IT MATTERS

It's easy to feel small or ordinary, like your life doesn't make much difference. But Jesus says otherwise. If you belong to Him, you are the salt of the earth—already placed to influence, preserve, and point people toward God. Lose that, and life grows bland. Live it out, and even small acts of love and truth can change everything.

🗣 THINK ABOUT IT

▶ Where in your life do you have the chance to add "flavor" through kindness, truth, or integrity?

_____
_____
_____
_____

▶ What might it look like to keep your saltiness strong in a world that often waters it down?

_____
_____
_____
_____

🫶 TRY THIS

Next time someone calls a person "THE SALT OF THE EARTH," you can say:

"Jesus actually said that about His followers—it means we're called to make a real difference in the world."

A simple phrase...
with a powerful mission behind it.

"THE SPIRIT IS WILLING, BUT THE FLESH IS WEAK"

(GOOD INTENTIONS... TOUGH FOLLOW-THROUGH)

YOU MIGHT'VE HEARD SOMEONE SAY...

"WELL, THE SPIRIT IS WILLING, BUT THE FLESH IS WEAK."

We usually say it with a laugh—when someone plans to wake up early to exercise but hits snooze, or when dessert looks too tempting after promising to "eat healthy." It's our way of admitting that good intentions don't always win.

But when Jesus said these words, it wasn't about diets or self-control—it was in the Garden of Gethsemane, the night before His crucifixion. As He prayed in agony, His disciples fell asleep. The phrase wasn't a joke—it was compassion. Jesus knew how real the struggle is between wanting to do right and having the strength to follow through.

[?] WHERE IT COMES FROM

The phrase comes from Matthew 26:41, when Jesus told His disciples in Gethsemane:

> "Watch and pray so that you will not fall into temptation. The spirit is willing, but the flesh is weak."

He had asked them to stay awake and pray with Him before His arrest, but they kept falling asleep. Jesus wasn't scolding them for being tired—He was warning them of *the danger of temptation*. He knew their hearts wanted to be faithful, but their *human weakness* could pull them down if they didn't **rely on prayer.**

⭐ STRENGTH BEYOND OURSELVES

Today, we use the phrase lightly, almost as a punchline. But in Scripture, it points to the very real battle between our intentions and our actions.

Wanting to do what's right isn't enough—we need God's strength to carry it out. The disciples had the desire to stand by Jesus, but without prayer, they didn't have the power. And the same is true for us.

🪴 WHY IT MATTERS

We all know the gap between our *best intentions* and our *actual follow-through.*

We want to love better, resist temptation, stay patient—but willpower alone eventually fails. That's why Jesus points us to prayer.

It's through **dependence on God's Spirit** that *weakness* becomes *strength*, and failure turns into growth.

Our weakness isn't the end of the story—it's an **invitation to lean on Him.**

🗣 THINK ABOUT IT

▸ Where in your life do your "good intentions" often collapse under weakness?

_____
_____
_____
_____
_____

▸ How could prayer help bridge the gap between wanting and doing?

_____
_____
_____
_____
_____

🫶 TRY THIS

Next time someone chuckles, "THE SPIRIT IS WILLING, BUT THE FLESH IS WEAK," you can say:

"Jesus actually said that—He was teaching that we need God's strength, not just good intentions."

A cliché about failure... that points us to real power.

CONCLUSION

The Bible has left its fingerprints everywhere—on our culture, our language, our art, even on the casual phrases we toss around without thinking. I've seen it firsthand, traveling around the world: no matter where you go, Scripture has found a way to shape the way people speak, dream, and live. That's not an accident—it's the mark of a book that isn't just ancient, but alive.

What makes the Bible so powerful is that it goes beyond ink on a page. It whispers in poetry, sings through music, anchors laws, comforts the broken, and sparks courage in movements for justice. It has connected people across centuries and cultures, giving us a shared heritage and a common language—even if we didn't realize where those words came from.

And that's what I hope this little journey has shown you: these "clichés" aren't empty. They're clues, little doorways back to God's story. They're everyday reminders that Scripture is still speaking, even in the grocery store, the office, or a late-night conversation with a friend.

So here's my encouragement: don't stop with this book. If you've recognized some of these phrases in your own life, take the next step. Go back to the Bible itself. Dig into the stories, the promises, the wisdom behind the words. You may be surprised at how fresh and personal it feels.

And when the chance comes up—at work, in class, around the dinner table—don't be afraid to share what you've discovered. A simple, "Did you know that phrase comes from the Bible?" might be all it takes to open the door to a deeper conversation.

My prayer is that these pages spark curiosity, yes—but more than that, that they lead you closer to the Author Himself. Because behind every saying, every story, every borrowed phrase is a God who still speaks today.

www.ingramcontent.com/pod-product-compliance
Lightning Source LLC
LaVergne TN
LVHW051636080426
835511LV00016B/2358